# William Prepares For Kindergarten

Written by William R. Johnson /williamgrows2307@aol.com

Illustrated by Jerrold Anderson

# William Prepares For Kindergarten

# Synopsis

A realistic story about a young boy named William preparing for Kindergarten. He is very nervous about Kindergarten. William's mother reminded him of some people who attended Kindergarten to help relax him. William learned a lesson from each of those important people that helped him prepare for the Kindergarten journey.

# William Prepares For Kindergarten

## Dedication:

Thanks to Mrs. Iris Montgomery-Ilori for the encouragement and direction in regards to putting this project together. To my beautiful mother, Gale Garrett, whose love and assistance are always greatly appreciated. To my brother Melvyn Jr. for being an inspiration even while being miles away. Dominique Merritt, thanks for your constant support and for being my best friend. Rewrite after rewrite, you continued to read without complaining. Your input has been truly invaluable. Mrs. Nadine Dillanado and the Mayo Elementary School Staff, your faith in my abilities transcended me to greater levels than even I thought I would reach. Mrs. Oreitha Benion, thanks for believing in me during my elementary school days at Crown and beyond. Many students at Mayo have been an inspiration. Smiles have brightened gloomy days, and the good cheer has kept my spirits lifted high. Thank you Mayo family for all you continue to teach me. Dashaun Harris, you have stood out among many students that helped with this book. Thanks for all your help, I know you will go far. To my classroom, Room 103, I am so proud of you and I love each and every one of you. You challenge me daily, but you reward me with your love and progress. Thanks to Pastor John F. Hannah at New Life Covenant church for consistently providing great Words to live by. They did not fall on deaf ears. Thanks to Bishop Gary B. Coach for the privilege of serving you at Refuge in New York. Each moment we have spent together made the reality of this book come alive.

----Love William R. Johnson

Copyright © 2009 by William R. Johnson

William R. Johnson

My name is William and I woke up this morning with a sparkle in my eyes.

William Prepares For Kindergarten

Today is the day I start Kindergarten. I am so nervous. I do not think the people there will like me.

In order to feel better, I thought about all the people my mom told me went to Kindergarten.

**William Prepares For Kindergarten**

My mom said, "William, I went to Kindergarten." I said, "Really?" My mom said, "I sure did."

I said, "Wow," and smiled. My mom is a teacher, so that made me feel really good.

## William Prepares For Kindergarten

Mom then told me, "Your Dad went to Kindergarten."
I said, "Really?" My mom said, "He surely did."

My dad is a chef. If my dad went to Kindergarten, I know it must be okay.

# William Prepares For Kindergarten

So, I smiled really big with excitement!

Mom continued by telling me, "Your sister Teresa went to Kindergarten too." I asked my mom, "Are you sure she went to Kindergarten too?"

She said, "Of course William. Teresa went to Kindergarten and she enjoyed it a lot." I began to get even more excited because my sister Teresa is a nurse.

Maybe that's where she got her start with caring about people.

**William Prepares For Kindergarten**

Kindergarten sounds like it might be better than I thought.

"Even your brother Melvyn Jr. went to Kindergarten." This was really going too far now. "My brother Melvyn Jr. went too?"

**William Prepares For Kindergarten**

When mom told me my brother Melvyn Jr. went to Kindergarten, I grew extremely happy. Mom said, "Yes William, he too went to Kindergarten."

My brother, Melvyn Jr. was in the Marines. My brother, Melvyn Jr. can do anything. If he went to Kindergarten, I know I can go.

William Prepares For Kindergarten

When I heard that all the most important people in my life went to Kindergarten, I was very excited. This is going to be the best time of my life.

I will not know many people at school, but I will try hard to meet people like my brother Melvyn Jr. taught me.

I will share my toys like
my sister Teresa taught me.

I will also show courtesy
(kindness) to others,
like my dad taught me.

I can't forget what my mom taught me.

She taught me that I should make new friends, learn something from my teacher, and remember that this is the first of many steps in my path to education.

Mom said, "Enjoy your Kindergarten year."

I am looking forward to Kindergarten now.

# William Prepares For Kindergarten

YES!

Now, I am off to Kindergarten!

# THE END

# Autobiography

William Robert Johnson

I was born in Chicago, Illinois on the west side of Chicago on July 23, 1973. I attended Blessed Sacrament and Crown Academy Elementary schools. I graduated from Holy Trinity High school on Chicago's North Side. My hobbies are writing, singing, entertaining, playing games, travelling, attending movies and plays, bowling, and driving the church bus. Four of my biggest accomplishments are: celebrating the birth of my daughter Victoria Love Johnson, completing a year-long tour in the Air Force's premier family entertainment showcase, Tops In Blue, which enabled me to travel around the world during my ten year military career as an Aircraft Analyst, Database Manager, Security Forces Augmentee, and a special duty assignment as a Recruiter. Teaching Social Studies to secondary school students in Ghana, Africa. Teaching English to Korean elementary school students in Seoul, Korea. I am currently an elementary school Kindergarten teacher at a prestigious school of choice, in Chicago's Bronzeville community. I am presently a student at Chicago State University pursuing a Master's degree in Special Education.

# William Prepares For Kindergarten

Made in the USA